to the home of

CAROL ECKLES –
WORKER OF DREAMS
2005

My friends
are my estate.
—*Emily Dickinson*

www.andrewsmcmeel.com
www.maryengelbreit.com

ISBN: 0-7407-0682-9

Illustrations by Mary Engelbreit
Design by Stephanie R. Farley

illustrated by
Mary Engelbreit

Andrews McMeel
Publishing
Kansas City

Cross-stitch created by Anna Chisholm and Gladys Chisholm Hooper

I don't know which I enjoy more, being a guest or having a guest (or two or three!) stay in my home. I love to keep a guest book, a log of happy times I have spent with good friends and family members. When I look through it, I am reminded of all the fun we've had at these grown-up slumber parties. Whether it's girlfriends from out of town or a family of four camped throughout the house, they all have stories to tell. I particularly enjoy watching my friend's children grow up. Their early signatures are outlines of their hands along with drawings of my various cats and dogs.

When I am lucky enough to be a guest at a friend's home, I make a mental note of all the things that make me feel welcome. Whether it's a carafe of ice water near my bed or a few good books and magazines to curl up with, I try to do the same when they are my guests. I love to find an extra pillow waiting for me (sometimes with a Snickers bar on top! Certainly beats a puny mint...) as well as a soft throw at the bottom of my bed. If I have time to sneak in a nap, a small soft blanket is all I need. That way I don't have to make up the bed!

Visiting my friend Terry Lee Bilsky, I was delighted to find her grandmother and aunt's cross-stitch hanging in her guest room. It was a gift from her Aunt Gladys who gave it to her when she moved to Vermont. Turns out it was a project her grandmother started some eighty years ago and as was the custom in their home, Aunt Gladys picked it up one day and finished it. It made me feel welcome as I am sure it will for you and your guests. So, make yourself at home, sit back and enjoy being my guest!

Mary

10-26-05

Carol, May your "Lake Home" be as welcoming to everyone as you are. Hope you have years of rest and pleasure here - Love, Cyrilla (The Nurse - not the nun)

Carol, it has been wonderful being here! There is good energy in this space. It's wonderful to habe the opportunity to "osamose" (sp?) it! Love, Jane 8-4-10

How many, many friendships
life's path has let me see;
I've kept a scrap of each
to make the whole of me.

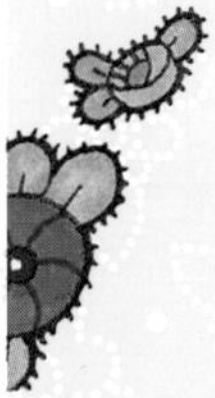

The world is full of friends
waiting to meet you.
—*Marion C. Garretty*

Treat your friends
as you do your pictures
and place them in their best light.
—*Jennie Jerome Churchill*

The beauty of the house is order,
the blessing of the house is contentment;
the glory of the house is hospitality.

—*Anonymous*

A house is a home
when it shelters the body
and comforts the soul.
—*Phillip Morris*

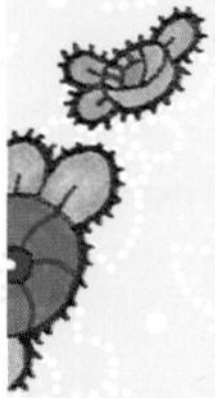

No matter where I se[illegible]y guests,
it seems th[illegible] my kitchen best.

[illegible]broidery Sampler

It takes a heap o' livin' in a house
t' make it home.

—*Edgar Albert Guest*

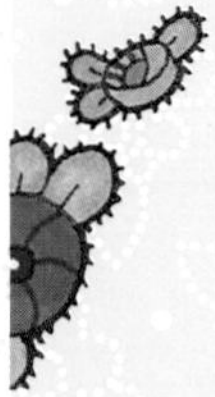

A friend is what
the heart needs all the time.
—*Henry Van Dyke*

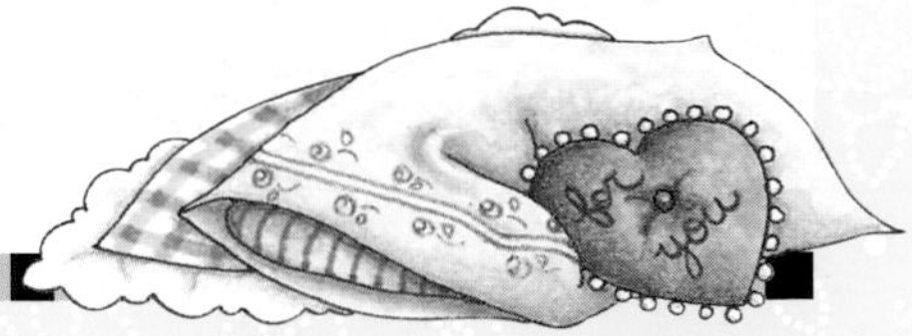

May you always find three welcomes in life:
in a garden during summer, at a fireside during winter,
and whatever the day or season
in the kind eyes of a friend.

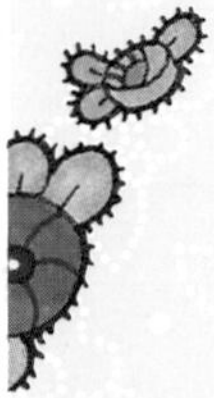

The ornament of a house
is the friends who frequent it.
—*Ralph Waldo Emerson*

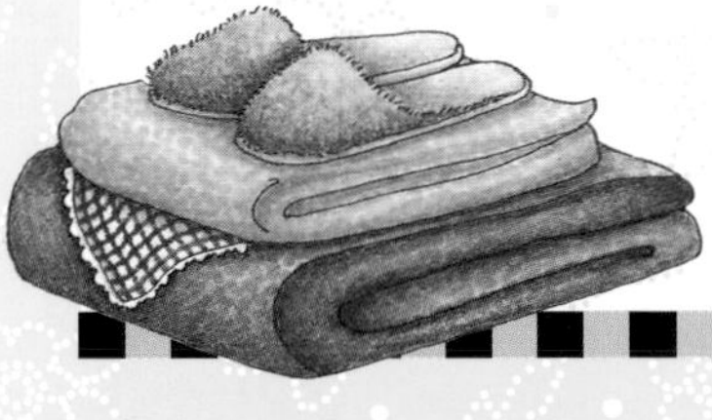

There's no place like home.

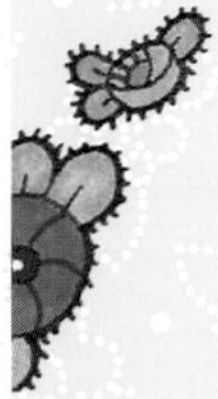

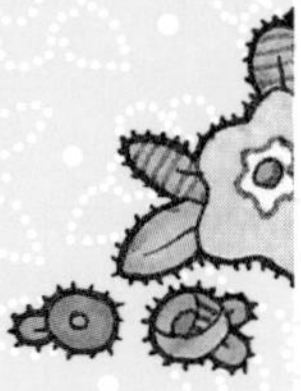

Have nothing in your house
that you do not know to be useful,
or believe to be beautiful.

—*William Morris*

To know someone here and there with whom you can feel
there is understanding in spite of distances
or thoughts unexpressed—
that can make this life a garden.

—Goethe

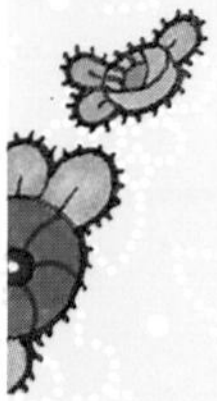

Ah, how good it feels!
The hand of an old friend.
—*Henry Wadsworth Longfellow*

Though we travel the world over to find the beautiful,
we must carry it with us, or we find it not.

—*Ralph Waldo Emerson*

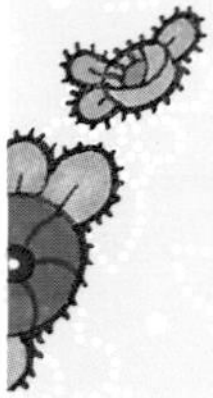

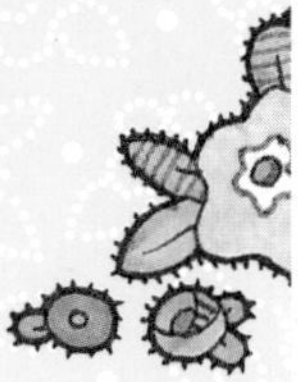

Home, the spot of earth supremely blest,
a dearer, sweeter spot than all the rest.
—*Robert Montgomery*

I do not understand how anyone
can live without one small place
of enchantment to turn to.

—Marjorie Kinnan Rawlings

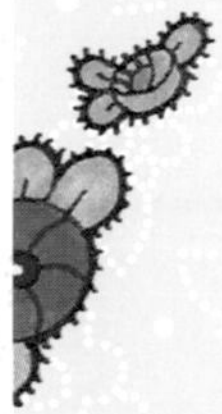

Be good to yourself,
be excellent to others,
and do everything with love.
—*John Wolf*

No matter where you go,
there you are.

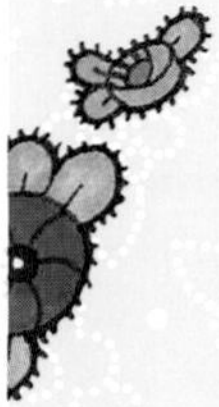

But every house where Love abides
And friendship is a guest,
Is surely home, and home-sweet-home;
For there the heart can rest.

—*Henry Van Dyke*

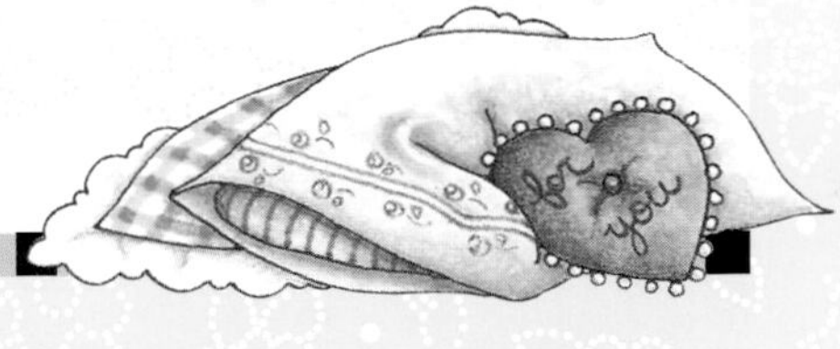

Let me live in a house by the road
and be a friend to man.
—*Embroidery Sampler*

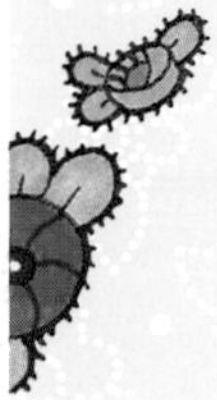

May you have warm words on a cold evening,
a full moon on a dark night,
and the road downhill all the way to your door.

Where we love is home.
Home that our feet may leave
but not our hearts.
—*Oliver Wendell Holmes*

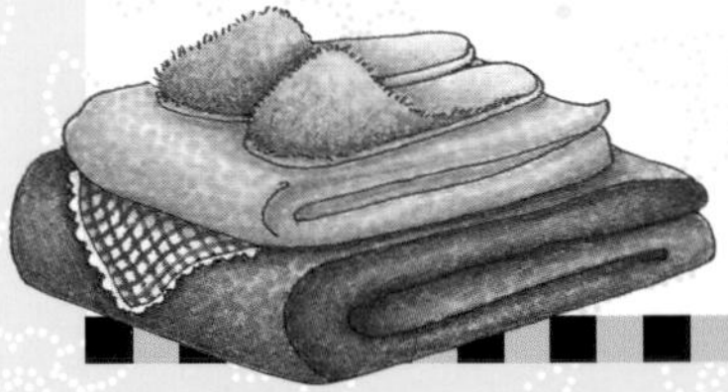

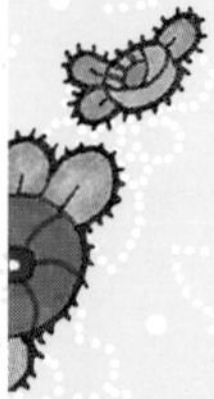

I love it—I love it;
and who shall dare
To chide me for loving that old armchair?
—*Eliza Cook*

Some people come into our lives,
make footprints on our hearts,
and we are never the same.

—*Anonymous*

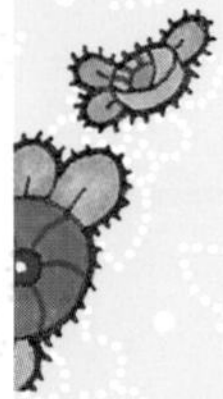

A friend can help to mend a heart,
boost you toward a brand new start, clown with carefree,
schoolgirl glee, share a quiet cup of tea.

—*Jan Miller Girando*

Always take the scenic route.

Home is an invention
on which no one has improved.
—*Ann Douglas*

A little Consideration,
a little Thought for Others,
makes all the difference.

—Eeyore the Donkey

Celebrate the happiness that friends are always giving,
making every day a holiday
and celebrate just living.

—*Amanda Bradley*

I love everything that's old;
old friends, old times, old manners,
old books, old wines.

—*Oliver Goldsmith*

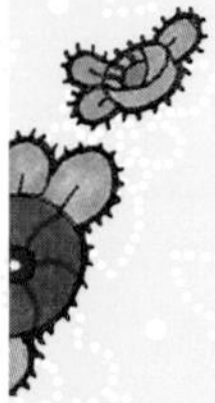

No matter what,
no matter where, it's always home,
if love is there.

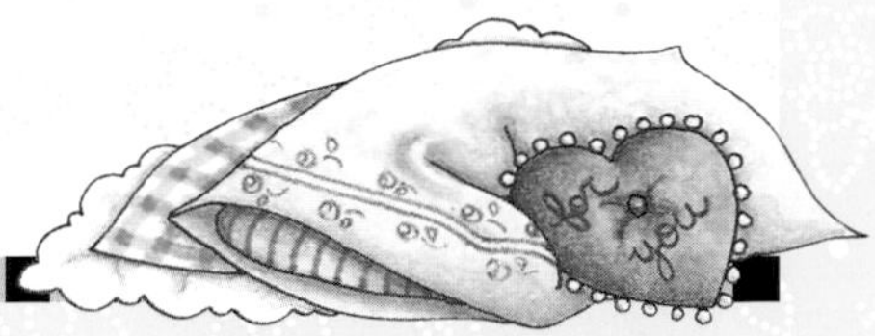

Keep company with those
who make you better.
—*English saying*

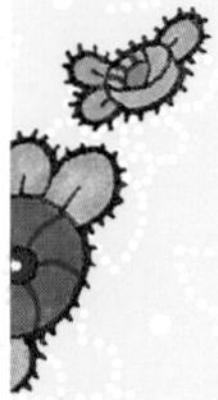

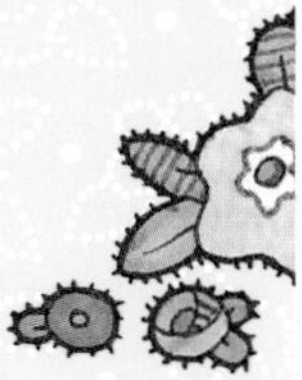

A good laugh is sunshine in a house.

—*William Makepeace Thackeray*

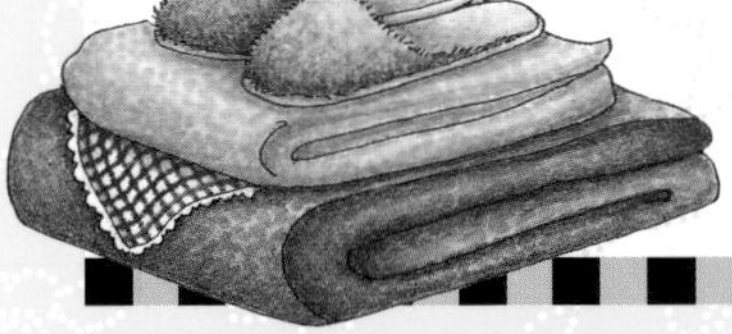

It was a delightful visit;
—perfect, in being much too short.
—Jane Austen

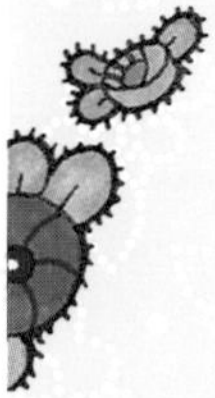

The pathway to a friend's house
is never very long.

Home is where the heart is.

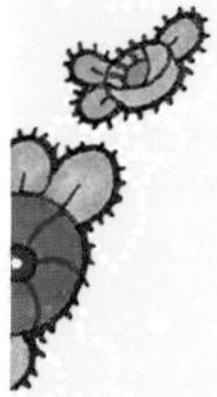

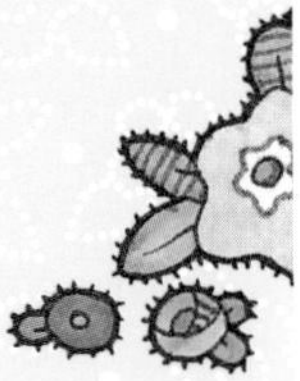

Come into my kitchen with me
While I prepare a cup of tea.
—*Embroidery Sampler*

Not fare well,
But fare forward, voyagers.
—*T.S. Eliot*

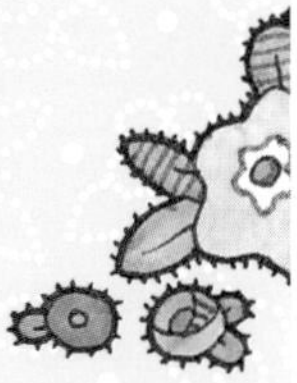

One's home is the safest refuge
to everyone.
—*Sir Edward Coke*

The manner of giving
is worth more than the gift.
—Pierre Cornielle

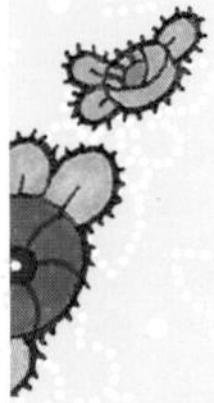

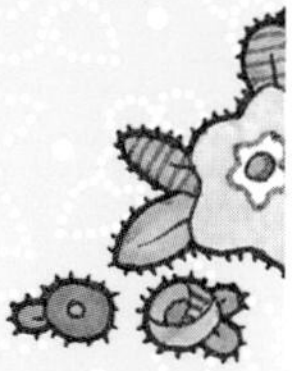

Small cheer and great welcome
makes a merry feast.
—*William Shakespeare*

Friends, books, a cheerful heart
and conscience clear
are the most choice companions
we have here.
—*William Mather*

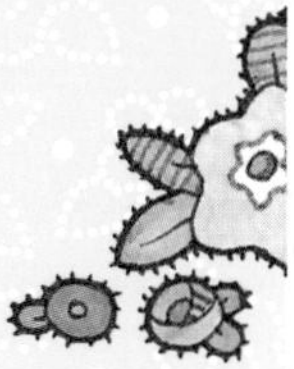

Home is heaven for beginners.
—*Charles Parkhurst*

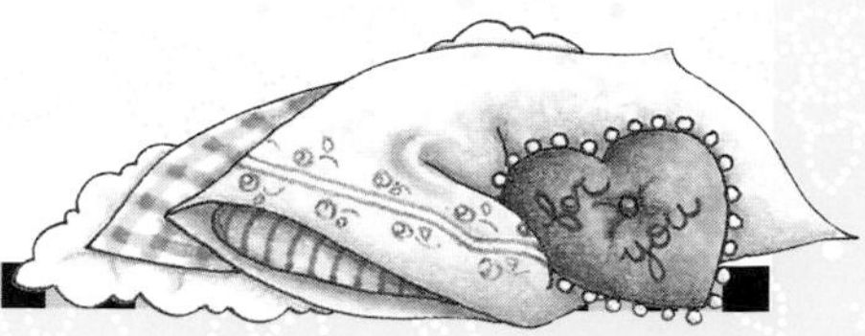

What is more agreeable
than one's home?
—*Cicero*

And until we meet again,
may God hold you
in the palm of His hand.

—Irish saying